Broken and Transformed Workbook

"Scripture quotations taken from the Amplified® Bible, Copyright © 1954, 1958, 1962, 1964, 1965, 1987 by The Lockman Foundation used by permission." (www.lockman.org)

Copyright © 2012 Kristi Lemley

All rights reserved.

ISBN- 13:978-1480139077

ISBN- 101480139076

Broken and Transformed Workbook

Moving beyond life's difficult times

Kristi Lemley

2012

Dedication

This workbook is dedicated to the many people that I have had the privilege to counsel, pray with, and minister to. May God bless you on your journey from brokenness to beauty!

TABLE OF CONTENTS

SECTION ONE   PAGE

Lesson 1	Can You Relate?	13
Lesson 2	What's Your Story?	17

SECTION TWO

Lesson 3	A Place Called Broken	23
Lesson 4	Finding Peace with God	29
Lesson 5	God Will Fight for You	37
Lesson 6	Identifying with Christ	41
Lesson 7	Life in the Word	49
Lesson 8	Forgiveness	55
Lesson 9	Battleground	62
Lesson 10	Take off Your Grave Cloths	74
Lesson 11	The Exchange	85

SECTION THREE

Lesson 12	Refreshing Times	95

LETTER FROM KRISTI   103

~ INTRODUCTION ~

This workbook accompanies the book entitled, *Broken and Transformed*. This workbook is not suited to complete without reading the book first or at the same time due to not everything in the book being covered in this workbook. This workbook is to assist in your own personal recovery at every point along your journey. Because of what you are experiencing, there may be instances where you need to spend more time in a given chapter. This is what I recommend instead of attempting to rush through the material just to complete it.

Take time completing the chapters. Do not rush through it even if you think you are ready for the next chapter. Take time in between the chapters so you can internalize the information that you have read. This will allow maximum benefit from the workbook.

It is my heartfelt prayer that this workbook assists in personalizing everything you read in the book to help you apply it directly to areas in your life. This workbook can be completed on your own or in a small group study where discussion can assist with healing. May God bless you on your journey!

SECTION ONE

ACTS 10:34, "AND PETER OPENED HIS MOUTH AND SAID: MOST CERTAINLY AND THOROUGHLY I NOW PERCEIVE AND UNDERSTAND THAT GOD SHOWS NO PARTIALITY AND IS NO RESPECTOR OF PERSONS."

~ Lesson 1 ~

Can you relate?

Prayer-

     Lord, help me to know I am not alone. Help me to know You are always with me and that You will never leave me. Help me to know I am not the only one who is going through something difficult. Help me to be more compassionate with others. In the name of Jesus,   Amen.

TESTIMONIES

What God did for Nancy, Ken, Kraig and me, He can and will do for you. Acts 10:34 says that God is no respecter of persons. What God has done for one, He will do for anyone who calls upon His name. God does not love one person more than another. You are just as important to God as anyone of the people in the testimonies. As you read the testimonies, do you notice what God did for each person? Did you notice the common theme of God showing up and delivering each person? He can and will do the same thing for you.

Another example proving that God is not a respecter of persons is found in Joshua chapter one. Moses had died and God told Joshua to rise up and take Moses' place. Joshua 1:5 states, "No man shall be able to stand before you all the days of your life. As I was with Moses, so I will be with you; I will not fail you or forsake you." The same words are spoken to you now, as God was with Nancy, Ken, Kraig, and me He is with you and will not fail you.

Kristi Lemley

What part of Kristi's testimony of *Broken by a past* were you able to relate to?

_____
_____
_____
_____

What part of Nancy's testimony of *Broken by divorce* were you able to relate to?

_____
_____
_____
_____

What part of Ken's testimony of *Broken by cancer* were you able to relate to?

_____
_____
_____
_____

What part of Kraig's testimony of *Broken by life* were you able to relate to?

_____
_____
_____
_____

Broken and Transformed Workbook

What part of Kristi's testimony *Broken by ministry* were you able to relate to?

_____
_____
_____
_____

Read I Corinthians 10:13. What does this scripture mean to you?

_____
_____
_____
_____
_____

How important is it to realize that other people go through difficult times also?

_____
_____

It is very important to realize that everyone goes through difficult times so that we do not get caught in a state of self-pity, self-blame, or self-abasement. Also, the Bible says that the enemy is the father of all lies (Acts 13:10). One lie the enemy tries to tell you is that you are the only one who understands. This is not true. Other people have gone through what you are currently going through. You are not the only one to deal with the situation. Maybe something you read in one of the testimonies helps you realize that you are not the only one or maybe you know someone personally who has gone through a similar situation. Don't allow the enemy to tell you that no one understands, because some people do. Jesus said in the Bible that you will have trials and tribulations, but that you will overcome because He did. (John 16:33)

What is one aspect you have learned in this lesson that was helpful?
_____
_____
_____
_____
_____

Prayer-

     Lord, thank you for showing me how much You love each one of Your children. Thank you for showing me how powerful You are, how much You care, and that I can trust You. Lord, You have my life in Your hands. Just as You took care of Nancy, Ken, Kraig, and Kristi I know You will take care of me. I love You Lord,   Amen.

~ Lesson 2 ~

What's Your Story?

Prayer-

     Lord, help me to be open to how You will speak to me. Help me to be honest with You and myself. I need You Lord. Thank you that you hear my prayers and respond. Help me to take off my mask and become real. In the name of Jesus,   Amen.

Write out your story. What is going on in your life that broke you?

_____

_____

_____

_____

_____

_____

_____

_____

_____

_____

_____

_____

Kristi Lemley

_____
_____
_____
_____
_____

How do you feel? _____
_____
_____
_____

What thoughts do you have? _____
_____
_____
_____

What fears rise up in you because of your situation? _____
_____
_____
_____

Have you experienced feeling this way before? _____
_____
_____
_____

How do you want to feel? _____
_____
_____
_____

Broken and Transformed Workbook

Re-read Psalm 91. What does it mean to you?

_____
_____
_____
_____
_____
_____
_____

What is one thing you have learned in this lesson that has been helpful?

_____
_____
_____
_____
_____

Prayer-

     Thank you Lord for helping me open up and become honest about what is going on in my life. It is not easy for me, but I know that you have me by the hand and are leading me, guiding me, and holding me up. I do not know where this situation will take me, but I know with You on my side I will make it through. I am ready to give you everything in order to move forward. Help me to not take it back to figure it all out on my own. I love you Lord,   Amen.

SECTION TWO

ZECHARIAH 4:6, "…NOT BY MIGHT, NOR BY POWER, BUT BY MY SPIRIT [OF WHOM THE OIL IS A SYMBOL], SAYS THE LORD OF HOSTS."

~ Lesson 3 ~

A Place Called Broken

Prayer-

  Lord, help me to accept where I am right now. I know nothing can change without me recognizing You are in control. The situation has overwhelmed me and I know I cannot go through it alone. Thank you for being with me in these difficult times. Help me to use wisdom in my daily life to do my part. In the name of Jesus,   Amen.

How has your situation impacted your ability to function?

_____

_____

_____

What part of your situation caused you to not be able to make sense of the situation?

_____

_____

_____

What part of your situation caused you to be subdued and humbled?

_____

_____

_____

Here is a list of things to do to help you on a daily basis to be able to function and continue to move forward:

1) Spend 20 minutes a day by yourself praying, reading your Bible, or singing praise music.

   Will this be difficult for you? _____

   Pick a time of day and begin praying every day at that time.

   What time have you chosen? _____

   What can you do to make sure you actually spend the time?

   _____
   _____
   _____

2) Ask others to pray for you.

   List three people that you can ask to pray for you.

   _____
   _____
   _____

3) Only tell a few close friends.

   List two trusted friends that you can talk with.

   _____
   _____

4) Go easy on yourself.

   Name two nice things you can do for yourself that help you feel calm and relaxed.

   _____
   _____

5) Only focus on important things.

   Make a to-do list at the beginning of the week of what needs to be done. (Include bills needing paid, grocery shopping, running errands, etc.)

   What needs to be done in the next couple of days?

   _____

   _____

6) Get enough sleep.

   Develop a nightly routine. Describe a nightly routine that will help you get to sleep.

   _____

   _____

7) Eat healthy meals.

   Keep track of what you are eating so you remember if you ate or not. What have you eaten today?

   _____

   _____

8) Exercise.

   Commit to exercising most days of the week. What types of activities can you do to exercise?

   _____

   _____

9) Do one activity a week that you enjoy.

List activities you like to do. _____

_____

_____

Pick one from the list above and plan it now. When will you do it?

_____

_____

When a person is broken, they have a decision to make- to run to God or away from God. I have addressed activities and things to do to help you on a daily basis, but a larger decision needs to be made. Will you run to God or away from Him? Are you running to God or away from Him? _____

What have you done to run to God? _____

_____

_____

What have you done to run away from God? _____

_____

_____

Sometimes we go back and forth from running to God and running away from God. What can you do to keep yourself from running away from God?

_____

_____

_____

Broken and Transformed Workbook

Read II Chronicles 20. What does it mean to you?

_____
_____
_____
_____

What do you need to stop doing that only God can do?

_____
_____
_____

Read Romans 8:35-39. What do these verses mean to you?

_____
_____
_____
_____
_____

What is one thing you have learned this lesson that has been helpful?

_____
_____
_____
_____

Kristi Lemley

Prayer-

Lord, thank you for Your love. Thank you that I can choose You and that You are right there helping me, taking care of me, and fighting for me. Help me to use the wisdom I have learned and apply it to my life. Help me to have balance and grace in my everyday life. Thank you for the hope that is beginning to raise in me that says I can make it through this. I love you Lord, Amen.

~ Lesson 4 ~

Finding Peace with God

Prayer-

    Lord, thank you for being here for me. Help me to allow You to go to the dark places in my life. I know You are my answer, so help me continue to turn to You everyday, even every moment. Help me to not be angry, but give You every emotion and thought. In the name of Jesus,   Amen.

How have you been calling out to God? _____

_____

_____

_____

Have you been contacting your people that are praying for you? _____

Are you angry at God? Why or why not? _____

_____

_____

Have you changed any activities since your situation occurred that involved spending time with God?

If yes, what? _____

_____

Do you think God could have prevented your situation? If yes, how? _____
_____
_____

What why questions have you asked? _____
_____
_____
_____

How do you feel right now? _____
_____
_____

Do you feel as if God has left you in some way? _____
_____
_____

Read Romans 8. What does this chapter mean to you?
_____
_____
_____
_____
_____

Broken and Transformed Workbook

Do you think God loves you? _____

We tend to view God's love for us by how we were shown love by our earthly father. Did you receive your earthly father's love growing up? _____

If yes, what did it look like? _____
_____
_____
_____

If no, how did that make you feel? _____
_____
_____
_____

Research the Bible. List other scriptures that address God's love.
_____
_____
_____
_____
_____

What is the most difficult part of accepting God's love?
_____
_____
_____

Kristi Lemley

Have you had an experience where you sensed God's love? Share it.

_____

_____

_____

_____

_____

_____

_____

When was the last time you were still and just received God's love?

_____

Read Psalm 46:10. What does it mean to you?

_____

_____

_____

_____

In order to be mindful of God, you have to take time to be still. This can be difficult with all the thoughts and emotions going on. When is the best time of the day (morning, afternoon, or night) for you to be still?

_____

When first practicing to be still, you may want to have praise and worship music playing. This can help you become focused. You may want to have a devotion book to get you focused on a subject. You may want to read a Psalm to help you ponder on the greatness of God. These activities will help you ease into being still.

Broken and Transformed Workbook

What could you begin with to help you be able to be still?

_____

_____

Where will you be still? Pick a few places that bring you peace. (Back deck, front porch, big chair in the living room, etc.)

_____

_____

Take time to be still right now. What is God speaking to your heart?

_____

_____

_____

_____

Do you sense God's presence? _____

Do you sense God revealing blessings to you? _____

What blessings do you currently recognize? _____

_____

_____

How often do you stop and think about the blessings in your life?

_____

When you are hurting, it is sometimes difficult to focus on positive areas and blessings in your life. I want to encourage you to keep a blessings journal. Write daily in this journal of all the blessings God is giving you. It is easier to remember when you write on a daily basis.

Read Hebrews 13:5-6. What does it mean to you?

___

When being mindful of God, you have to know that He wants to help you. What ways has God helped you in this difficult time? ___

___

Read Matthew 11:28-30. What does it mean to you?

___

How can God help you rest?

___

Broken and Transformed Workbook

Read Jeremiah 29:11. What does it mean to you?

_____
_____
_____
_____
_____

What plans do you have for your life? _____

_____
_____
_____

What plans do you sense God has for your life? _____

_____
_____
_____
_____

What keeps you from trusting God completely? _____

_____
_____
_____
_____

Search for more scriptures on trusting God. List at least five.

_____
_____

What is one thing you have learned this lesson that has been helpful?

_____
_____
_____
_____

Prayer-

     Thank you Lord that You have a plan for my life. Help me to trust You, even if I cannot see the next step. Thank you for Your love, presence, and peace. I cannot move forward without You and I am glad I don't have to. You are my strength and strong tower that I can run to. You are my saving grace. I love You Lord,   Amen.

~ Lesson 5 ~

God Will Fight for You

Prayer-

    Thank you Lord that I am not in this alone. Thank you that You are fighting for me and carrying me. Help me to sense Your presence today. Help me to trust that the battle is already won and all I have to do is stand firm in You. In the name of Jesus,   Amen.

Read II Chronicles 20:15-17. What does it mean to you?

_____

_____

_____

_____

_____

God is fighting for you. Do you see God fighting for you? _____

How is God showing you He is fighting for you? _____

_____

_____

How have you been fighting for yourself? _____

_____

_____

Do you need to quit trying to fight in your own strength? _____

What do you need to cease doing in order to allow God to fight for you?

_____

_____

_____

Who are you angry at and why are you angry at them? _____

_____

_____

_____

_____

Ephesians 6:12 states our war is not with people but with evil. When you are broken it is easy to become offended. I want to encourage you to not become easily offended at this time. You may perceive things people say differently than what they mean by their words. You may have misunderstandings with people or forget conversations that result in problems. Just remember, they are not your enemy. Allow God to work in your life and the lives of other people around you. When you expend energy on fighting other people, you are not allowing God to fight for you.

Do you need to let go of some things that have been misunderstandings, if so what?

_____

_____

_____

Broken and Transformed Workbook

What can you do to have peace with people in your life?

_____

_____

_____

Having peace with people is so important however, finding peace with God is the most important aspect of all. God is your only answer that brings peace and life. This does not mean you will never have questions nor do everything right.

Do you find yourself angry with God? _____

What has God done that makes you angry at Him? _____

_____

_____

_____

Do you feel guilty for being angry at God? _____

Do you think you are the only person to ever become angry at God? _____

If you are angry at God, pray and ask God to help you:

    Know His love.

    Be mindful of every blessing.

    Be still.

    Enter His rest.

    Trust Him.

    Allow Him to fight for you.

    Have peace with Him, others, and yourself.

Kristi Lemley

What is one thing you have learned this lesson that is helpful?

_____

_____

_____

_____

Prayer-

    Thank you Lord for Who You are. You are great and mighty! I know I have a ways to go, but my hope is rising. I may not be able to see the changes yet, but I know and trust they will come. You are my everything. I know with You on my side all things are possible. I love You Lord,   Amen.

~ Lesson 6 ~

Identifying with Christ

Prayer-

     Lord, help me to know You understand and know what I am going through. Some days it is all I can do to get out of bed and make it through the day. Help me to listen for your direction and sense Your love for me. Give me peace that surpasses understanding. Thank you that You hear my cries for help. In the name of Jesus, Amen.

Have you ever believed that life should be easier since you are a Christian? _____

Read John 16:33. What does it mean to you?

_____
_____
_____
_____

Read Philippians 2:6-8. What are your thoughts of Jesus stripping Himself of all privileges to become a servant and suffer death?

_____
_____
_____

How hard would this be for you? _____

What does this say about the love of Jesus for you? _____

_____

_____

Read Matthew 4:1. Jesus was tempted and tried. Do you notice who tempted and tried Him? Who?

_____

The Holy Spirit let Jesus into the wilderness for a time of fasting and prayer. However, it was the devil that tested and tried Jesus. Is your situation such that you were doing the right thing, yet it created more problems for you and a time of trial and testing? If so, that can create multiple negative feelings and responses. Do you currently feel-

    Betrayed   _____

    Lonely   _____

    Exhausted   _____

Read Hebrews 4:15. In what other ways are you currently suffering like Christ experienced? (Rejected, lied about, physically abused, misunderstood) _____

_____

_____

How does it make you feel knowing that Jesus knows how you feel?

_____

_____

_____

Broken and Transformed Workbook

Does it make you more confident in Him? _____

What keeps you from boldly, fearlessly, and confidently going to the throne and asking for mercy and help?

_____
_____
_____
_____

Have you ever had an experience when God showed up just in time? Explain.

_____
_____
_____
_____

Read I Corinthians 10:13. Is there anything you are being tempted to do that you know you shouldn't? What is it? _____

Are your thoughts negative? _____

Are your emotions overwhelming? _____

I love the last part of this scripture; that God provides the way out. Himself! Even though you are going through a time of testing and trial, God will show you what you need to do to make it through this difficult time. He is the way, truth, and life.

Are you doing anything right now that is turning to something or someone else rather than God? If yes, who or what? _____

Read John 1:12. What does this mean to you?

What privileges come with being a child of a King?

Romans 8:17 states if we are His children then also His heirs. What does it mean to be an heir?

What does it mean for you to be an heir of God?

What does it look like in a tangible way?

Broken and Transformed Workbook

Do you need to identify with Christ in order to forgive yourself? _____

Did you create the situation you are in? _____

Even though you may not have created the situation, have you made the situation worse? If yes, how?

_____

_____

_____

Read the following scriptures and comment on what they mean to you.

Romans 8:23 _____

_____

_____

_____

Romans 5:8 _____

_____

_____

_____

Psalm 103:9-12 _____

_____

_____

_____

Romans 8:1 _____

_____

_____

_____

Kristi Lemley

Acts 13:38 _____

_____

_____

_____

Are you angry with yourself? _____

Do you "beat" yourself up? _____

Do you need to accept forgiveness for your sins? _____

Steps to forgiveness

1)   Repent of sin

2)   Ask God for forgiveness

3)   Pray and ask God to help you receive His mercy and grace

4)   Make sure you cease the behavior

5)   Keep reading scriptures on forgiveness

It may take time for you to accept and sense God's forgiveness, but do not give up! Keep praying and pressing into God.

Is there anyone who may try to remind you of your sin? _____

What will they do to remind you? _____

_____

_____

How will you handle that person? _____

_____

Broken and Transformed Workbook

Read Mark 5:36. What does it mean to you? _____

_____

_____

_____

Overhearing, but ignore and keep on believing. Do not let anyone keep you in guilt, but know you have been forgiven. It may take others time before they forgive you, but that is between them and God. (As long as you have ceased the behavior and are attempting to change, otherwise it becomes more difficult for people to forgive if you continue with the same behaviors.)

What can you do to make sure you act in accordance with God's Word and do not make the situation worse?

_____

_____

_____

The last issue with identifying with Christ is to identify with the Word of God.

Read John 1:1, 14. What do these verses mean to you?

_____

_____

_____

_____

Read the Word and allow it to speak to you.

Identifying with Christ is very important. You cannot trust Him without first identifying with Him. Have you ever identified with Christ before? Have you accepted Him as your Lord and Savior? _____

If yes, GREAT! If not, do you want to? _____

What is one thing you have learned this lesson that has been helpful?
_____
_____
_____
_____

Prayer-

    If you have not accepted Christ and want to accept Him as your Savior, then pray this simple prayer- *Lord, I admit I am a sinner. I believe that Jesus came and died on the cross for my sins. I confess that I need Him in my life daily. Please come into my life today and help me. Thank you Jesus.*   AMEN

~ Lesson 7 ~

Life in the Word

Prayer-

    Thank you Lord that You know me. Thank you that You have shown me the way to truth and freedom. My answer is found in You. Help me to receive all that You want to show me, speak to me, and give to me. In the name of Jesus,

                                                       Amen.

Read II Timothy 3:16. What does this mean to you?

_____

_____

_____

_____

Do you believe every scripture comes for God? _____

Do you believe God's Word is relevant for today? _____

Do you believe God's Word is relevant for your life? _____

Do you believe God's Word is alive? _____

Kristi Lemley

Are you open to everything that God wants to speak to you? If yes, why? If no, why not?

___

Read Hebrews 4:12. What does this mean to you?

___

Read Psalm 119:50. What does this mean to you?

___

Jeremiah 1:12 states that God watched over His Word to perform it. What scriptures has God been speaking to you? ___

___

Read Romans 10:17. What does this mean to you?

___

Broken and Transformed Workbook

In what areas is your faith lacking? _____
_____
_____

I want to encourage you to seek out 10 scriptures in every area that your faith needs a boost.

Area _____   Area _____   Area _____

_____   _____   _____

_____   _____   _____

_____   _____   _____

_____   _____   _____

_____   _____   _____

_____   _____   _____

_____   _____   _____

_____   _____   _____

_____   _____   _____

_____   _____   _____

Read Romans 4. How would you have responded if you were Abraham?

_____
_____

What area (s) in your life feels dead right now? _____
_____
_____

The best way to bring life is to read the Bible and allow it to change your negative thoughts into positive thinking. How you think will impact how you feel.

Read Romans 12:2. What does this mean to you?
_____
_____
_____
_____

How can you change your schedule to increase the probability of reading your Bible daily?
_____
_____
_____
_____

Do you have a comfortable place to read your Bible? Where?
_____

Do you have a concordance or other books that can help you find scriptures or help you understand what you are reading? _____

If no I encourage you to ask your pastor or a trusted friend for a recommendation and purchase a Bible concordance and Bible commentary. When do you plan on asking them? _____

Broken and Transformed Workbook

At the end of the chapter in the book, there are multiple scriptures listed. Which scriptures do you relate to and are the most helpful right now? _____

_____
_____
_____
_____
_____
_____
_____
_____
_____
_____
_____

I encourage you to write down some scriptures on note cards and carry them around with you. When you need them, pull them out and read them. This will help keep your thoughts focused on God and His Word. The Word of God brings life. It can change your whole way of thinking for the day.

What is one thing you have learned that has been helpful this lesson?

_____
_____
_____
_____

Kristi Lemley

Prayer-

Thank you Lord that Your Word brings life, light, and love. Your Word uplifts, encourages, and refreshes me. I do not know where I would be without You. Help me to remember Your Word in the difficult moments and lead me to scriptures that I need. I know I can trust You Lord. Help me to stand firm on Your promises. I love You Lord, Amen.

~ Lesson 8 ~

Forgiveness

Prayer-

    Help me Lord to remember how Your great love has delivered me and saved me. I know that I am not perfect and make mistakes. Help me to offer that same grace to others. Help me Lord to be honest about forgiveness and the need to forgive. Help me to want to forgive. Help me to give You all my anger, hurt, and disappointment. Thank you Lord that Your mercies are new every morning and that You are patient with me. In the name of Jesus, Amen.

Forgiving others is a necessary step to wholeness. You may not think you need to forgive anyone, but keep reading. Ask God to show you if there is anyone you need to forgive. Be open. Be honest.

Do you need to forgive someone? _____ Y   _____ N

I realize that as you are reading this, you may not be ready to forgive. You may have a sense of "I deserve to be angry" attitude. If you have been hurt on purpose, then those feelings are real and normal. If your husband hits you or you have been raped, then you are justified in feeling this way. I am not saying that those feelings are wrong or not normal. However, those feelings are not healthy to keep. There comes a certain point that in order to move forward, you are going to need to pray and ask God to help you WANT to forgive.

This lesson is not intended to minimize what you have experienced or to invalidate your pain. Your feelings of anger, fear, shame, or betrayal need to be addressed and processed. However, I have been where you are and it is important to not remain stagnant or you will become stuck. Chances are you are stuck right now and that is why you are using this workbook.

What does forgiveness mean?

1. Letting go of the pain, resentment, bitterness that was caused by the person who hurt you.

2. No longer wanting to punish the person who hurt you.

Who do you need to forgive? _____
_____
_____

Forgiveness for what?
_____
_____
_____
_____

Read these scriptures and write what they mean to you.

Romans 3:23 _____
_____
_____

Matthew 6:12, 14-15_____
_____
_____

Broken and Transformed Workbook

Matthew 18:21-22 _____

_____

_____

Ephesians 4:26-27, 32_____

_____

_____

Hebrews 12:14-15 _____

_____

_____

Luke 23:34 _____

_____

_____

I John 2:9-11 _____

_____

_____

Luke 1:76-79 _____

_____

_____

II Peter 1:9 _____

_____

_____

Luke 6:35-38 _____

_____

_____

Kristi Lemley

Mark 11:25-26 _____

_____

_____

Romans 4:7-8 _____

_____

_____

Colossians 3:13 _____

_____

_____

What area of forgiveness is most difficult for you? _____

_____

_____

Are you struggling with, "but what the person did was horrible?" _____

Do you have an, "I don't care attitude" about you not being forgiven if you don't forgive others?

_____

Are you refusing to forgive? Is yes, what is your argument? _____

_____

_____

Pray and ask God to help you want to forgive. If you do want to forgive, pray and ask God to help you forgive. Being able to forgive is a process and definitely takes divine intervention. It is human nature to not want to forgive, but divine to forgive.

Broken and Transformed Workbook

What scripture above is helpful for you to forgive someone?
_____

Carry this scripture around with you so when you begin to think about how angry you are, you can read the scripture and pray to let the negative feelings go.

What can you do to live at peace with the person who wronged you?
_____
_____
_____

How does holding onto anger, resentment, and bitterness affect your life?
_____
_____
_____

What have you allowed yourself to do because you did not forgive?
_____
_____
_____

Hurting people hurt people. How is this true for the person who hurt you?
_____
_____
_____

Kristi Lemley

How would your life- emotionally, relationally, and spiritually, be different if you completely forgave?

_____
_____
_____
_____
_____

Do you have headaches, stomach aches, acid reflux, sleeping problems, high blood pressure, body aches, or any other physical problems? _____

List all medical problems since your situation happened.

_____
_____
_____

Did you have any medical conditions before your situation that have gotten worse since the situation occurred? _____

_____
_____

Pray and ask God to help you forgive. I have experienced people who would come to the altar for healing and yet they still were holding onto unforgiveness. When they gave up the unforgiveness, many times, they were healed. This is not the case in every situation or even most situations, however, it has happened enough for me to make the correlation.

Broken and Transformed Workbook

Do you need to accept forgiveness for yourself? _____

Know that Jesus died for all. For you, for me, and for the person who hurt you. In the natural realm, what one person did can seem worse than what another person did. However, in the spiritual realm, it is all sin. Sin brings about a break in relationship with God.

Spend more time in this area if you are struggling. Look up more scriptures on forgiveness and keep reading them until they settle in your spirit.

Forgiveness is a process, not a one word deal. Allow the grace of God to help you want to forgive and then to help you to completely forgive.

What is one thing you have learned in the lesson that has been helpful?
_____
_____
_____
_____

Prayer-

    Lord, help me to want to forgive and move beyond my anger and hurt. Help me daily to continue to give it all to You instead of hanging on to it. Remind me of Your Word and grace so that I may extend mercy and grace to those that have harmed me. Continue to speak truth to my heart that I would be open to Your leading and prompting. You are the way, truth, and life. I love you Lord,

                                              Amen.

~ Lesson 9 ~

Battleground

Prayer-

     Lord, the times are tough and some days are so difficult, but I know help is coming. Your Word says to submit myself to You, stand firm, and the devil will flee. Lord, help me to stand firm. Give me strength to stand on Your Word with peace, faith, and trust. In the name of Jesus, Amen.

Read James 4:7. What does it mean to you?

_____

_____

_____

The battleground is where you stand firm against the enemy while God does the battling. The important part of this is that you keep your eyes on God even if you do not see anything actively changing.

Read Ephesians 6:11-13. What does this mean to you?

_____

_____

_____

_____

Broken and Transformed Workbook

Do you notice we war not with flesh and blood? People are not your problem but evil is.

Read Ephesians 6:14-17. This reveals the armor of God.

How can you secure truth in your life? _____
_____
_____

How can you walk in integrity? _____
_____
_____

What do you need to do to walk in peace? _____
_____
_____

How can you increase your faith? _____
_____
_____

What do you need to think on to keep your thoughts positive and to know who you are in Christ?
_____
_____
_____

How can you speak the Word of God more? _____
_____
_____

When was the last time you praised God? _____

How often do you break out and praise God? _____

Read Psalm 100:4. What does it mean to you?

_____
_____
_____
_____

Focusing on God makes you take your eyes off of yourself and your problems and put them on Him. When you speak about how big God is, then everything else fades away. An activity that can help you praise God is to begin with A and go to Z using words to describe God.

In John 13:34, Jesus states we are to love others. When you reach out to others, you forget about yourself.

Read Romans 12:21. What does it mean to you?

_____
_____
_____
_____

Broken and Transformed Workbook

How can you walk in love and reach out to others? _____
_____
_____
_____
_____
_____

Read Isaiah 55:11. What does this mean to you?

_____
_____
_____
_____

Read Proverbs 18:21. What do you say throughout the day? _____
_____
_____
_____
_____

Begin paying attention to your words and see if they bring life or destruction.

Write down comments you made today that you can remember?

_____
_____
_____

Kristi Lemley

Write down scriptures that you find strength, comfort, peace or help with.

_____

_____

Read Philippians 4:8. What does this mean to you?

_____

_____

_____

_____

What you think will determine how you feel.

What thoughts do you need to stop thinking? _____

_____

_____

_____

_____

How can you work on stopping those thoughts? _____

_____

_____

_____

_____

One technique is called thought stopping. When you begin to have a negative thought, tell yourself stop, and replace it with a positive thought. Continue doing this until it becomes a habit.

Broken and Transformed Workbook

Read Ephesians 6:18. What does it mean to you?

_____
_____
_____
_____
_____

What is something you need to pray about but haven't yet? _____

_____
_____
_____
_____

Do you believe God hears your prayers? Why or why not? _____

_____
_____
_____
_____

Do you believe God answers prayers? _____

Read Mark 11:24. What does it mean to you?

_____
_____
_____
_____

Read James 1:3-4. What does it mean to you?

_____

_____

_____

_____

Allow your trial to bring you closer to God not create a hard heart or bad attitude towards Him. Have you learned that being around someone who is always complaining, angry, or feeling sorry for themselves is exhausting? You do not want to become that person. Do you tend to want everyone's attention or sympathy? _____

What can you do to not wallow in your pain? _____

_____

_____

Read Nehemiah 8:10. What does this mean to you?

_____

_____

_____

Joy is not based on your circumstance, but your view. What can you do on a daily basis to increase your joy?

_____

_____

_____

Broken and Transformed Workbook

Read James 1:5. What does this mean to you?

_____
_____
_____
_____

Do you tend to live by wisdom or your emotions? _____

How can you increase using wisdom instead of reacting emotionally?

_____
_____
_____

One way to learn to react using wisdom instead of emotions is to focus on what you know, not how you feel!

It is important to know how you feel, but not to be controlled by your feelings. Take time to make decisions.

How can you wait to make important decisions until you know or sense you are making a good decision?

_____
_____
_____

Read Proverbs 4:23. What does this mean to you?

_____
_____
_____
_____

Kristi Lemley

What is in your heart right now? (Anger, fear, resentment, insecurity, jealousy, etc)

_____
_____
_____

How can you guard your heart? _____

_____
_____
_____

Read Jeremiah 17:9-10. What does it mean to you?

_____
_____
_____
_____

Read Psalm 46:10. What does this mean to you?

_____
_____
_____
_____

How can you be still? _____

_____
_____

Broken and Transformed Workbook

What do you need to do to be still daily? _____

_____

_____

What have you learned from being still before? _____

_____

_____

What is the most important part of God's character that you need to know and meditate on right now?

_____

_____

Read John 14:27. What does this mean to you?

_____

_____

_____

_____

The Amplified Bible states to stop allowing ourselves to be agitated and disturbed. It also states to not permit ourselves to be fearful, intimidated, cowardly, or unsettled. What are you currently doing, thinking, or saying that agitates, causes fear, or unsettles you? _____

_____

_____

_____

Read Psalm 34:14. What does this mean to you?

_____

_____

_____

_____

Peace is not something that just comes or falls on you. You have to seek it, crave it, and pursue it. What can you do in order to have more peace? _____

_____

_____

Ask God right now to show you what is keeping you from having peace. What comes to your mind?

_____

_____

_____

Read II Corinthians 12:9. What does it mean to you?

_____

_____

_____

_____

What areas in your life do you need God's grace and mercy? _____

_____

How can you become more aware on a daily basis of God's grace?

_____

_____

_____

_____

When we are weak, God is strong! The battle continues all around you. You know the battle is the Lord's, but you are on the battleground. You cannot escape the battleground, but you can escape defeat. Do all that you can and allow God to do the rest. Stand fast and see the deliverance of the Lord!

What is one thing you have learned this lesson that has been helpful?

_____

_____

_____

_____

Prayer-

    Lord, thank you that the ultimate battle has already been won. Thank you for all the weapons of warfare that You give me. Help me to be mindful of the weapons and stand strong while on the battleground. I know Your Word says that I will tread upon serpents and scorpions and nothing shall in anyway harm me and I thank you for that protection and authority in Your name. I know my deliverance is coming! I love You Lord,   Amen.

~ Lesson 10 ~

Take off your Grave Cloths

Prayer-

    Thank you Lord that You continue to help me, be with me, and guide me. There are days that I am not sure if I can make it, yet You show up and get me through it. I do not know where I would be without You and I am so thankful that I do not have to find out. Help me to continue on this journey with strength, determination, and love. You alone are my answer! In the name of Jesus,   Amen.

Once you have been broken, you have to then be transformed. Transformation is a process. During this time, you will begin to process what has actually happened, what you have learned, and how to move forward.

Read John 11. There are two main points that I want to address.

1)   It took belief that Jesus could raise the dead.

Do you believe that God can give your situation new life? _____

Do you believe He can bring life back into you? _____

It is imperative that you believe He is the giver of life. John 10:10 talks about how the thief tears down, but that Jesus gives life.

2)   When God calls you forth, arise.

Jesus called Lazarus out of death into life. The same will happen to you. When God begins to lead you, you must begin to follow. Do not remain in your brokenness. This is a point that cannot be missed. So many times God begins to give new life to broken people, but they never take off the burial cloths. When the burial cloths remain on, the person cannot fully receive the new life. This is where most people become stuck. They begin to feel better and their situation begins to change, so they pull back from God because they are no longer so desperate for Him.

Why take off your grave cloths?

1) When you keep the grave cloths on, you remain in bondage.

Read John 8:32, 36. What do they mean to you?

_____
_____
_____
_____

Ask God right now what part of your situation is keeping you in bondage. What comes to your mind? (Disappointment, fears, grief, shame, embarrassment)

_____
_____
_____

What will happen if you continue to allow your situation to keep you in bondage?

_____
_____
_____
_____

Read Galatians 5:1, 3. What do these verses mean to you?

_____
_____
_____
_____

Lazarus needed help taking off the grave cloths. Do you need help taking off yours? _____

What or who can help you? _____

_____

2)   When you do not take off your grave cloths, you are unable to see where God is leading you or hear what He is speaking to you.

Read Jeremiah 7:23. What does this mean to you?

_____
_____
_____
_____

Take time right now and be still. Ask God to reveal to you if you are missing seeing Him or hearing Him.

_____
_____

Are you allowing a hard heart, bitterness, or resentment to continue? _____

Broken and Transformed Workbook

Do you have an attitude towards people? _____

Are your emotions getting the best of you? _____

What do you need to do in order to keep communication lines open between you and God?

_____

_____

3) When you refuse to take off your burial cloths it restricts your movement.

Can a person move when they are all tied up? _____

Brokenness can cause people to become self-centered and very selfish. "I have to protect myself. I have to take care of me. If I don't watch out for myself, no one else will." These are statements that are made over and over.

How are you being selfish or self-centered? _____

_____

_____

Do you think this is impacting your ability to reach out and help others? _____

How? _____

_____

_____

_____

Kristi Lemley

If taking off the grave cloths were easy, most people would do it every time. However, this is the part that people remain stuck in and never move beyond. Why? Here are the reasons why people do not take off their grave cloths: fear, you think God has not shown up, feeling stuck, and self-pity.

1) Fear

Read Job 3:25. What does it mean to you?

_____
_____
_____
_____

What fears do you have? _____
_____

Read II Timothy 1:7. What does it mean to you?

_____
_____
_____
_____

What do you need to do in order to overcome your fears? _____
_____
_____

Broken and Transformed Workbook

Read Hebrews 2:15. What does it mean to you?

_____

_____

_____

_____

You must face what you are afraid of in order to overcome it. What is in darkness has power over you. Once it is brought to the light, it loses its ability to control you. How did Jesus handle people who wanted to keep Him in fear?

Read Mark 5:36. Overhearing but ignoring! Keep believing that God has you in the palm of His hand. What can you do to ignore certain voices? _____

_____

_____

_____

2)	God hasn't shown up.

Sometimes your situation is improving but not drastically. You wonder if God has actually shown up. What will it take for you to realize that God is working for you and has not forgotten about you?

_____

_____

_____

Read Isaiah 43:19. What does this mean to you?

_____

_____

_____

_____

How has God shown up in your life and situation? _____

_____

_____

_____

If you think God has not shown up, do you feel stronger than when the situation first started? Do you feel hope? Has someone contacted you to say they are praying for you? If you answered yes to any of the questions, then God has shown up. It is all about perception.

Read Proverbs 3:5-6. What does this mean to you?

_____

_____

_____

_____

Are you trying to make sense of things in order to feel like God is helping you?

_____

_____

Broken and Transformed Workbook

If you are reading this right now, God has already been in your situation because He led me to write these words for you to be reading them at this time. God's timing is perfect.

3) Do you feel stuck?

It becomes easy to just survive instead of living when you are going through a difficult time. Do you feel like you are just surviving? _____

Read Hebrews 6:11-12. What does it mean to you?

_____
_____
_____
_____

You have to change your mindset from surviving and just making it to a mindset of, "I will make it through this and be victorious!" How can you do this? Talk to a trusted friend. Talk with your pastor. Read scriptures on being victorious.

What do you need to do to live, really live again? _____

_____

4) Self-pity

Have you ever made the statement, "This is too hard?" Are you making this statement right now? _____

What do you find "too hard" right now? _____
_____
_____

Did you know self-pity is really pride? When you begin to focus on how everything is so bad, unfair, etc. then you are setting your situation up above God.

Read Psalm 11:2. What does it mean to you?

_____
_____
_____
_____

I know this scripture may be difficult right now, but so is feeling empty. The only way to be able to take the grave cloths off completely is to let go of self-pity.

I want to encourage you by saying God knows what you have been through. He knows how you were hurt and how it has impacted your life. But I also know He wants to help you if you let Him.

Read Romans 12:19. What does this mean to you?

_____
_____
_____
_____

Broken and Transformed Workbook

God is a God of justice and nothing that has happened has gone unnoticed.

Read I Corinthians 10:13. What does it mean to you?

_____

_____

_____

_____

Everyone has felt sorry for themselves at one time or another. The important point is to not remain there. I want to encourage you right now to ask God to reveal to you if you are feeling sorry for yourself. What do you sense God speaking to you? _____

_____

The truth is we all have difficult times and Jesus even told us we would. It is how we move forward in those difficult times that determine our destiny.

Read Mark 8:34-35. What does it mean to you?

_____

_____

_____

_____

You have to take off your grave cloths in order to continue to move forward. Once you do, you will experience your ashes turning into beauty. Are you ready to allow the bad to drop and make a rainbow from the storm?

Kristi Lemley

What is one thing you have learned this lesson that has been helpful?

_____

_____

_____

_____

Prayer-

      Lord I know in order to move forward, I have to let go of my past. Help me to be ready and willing to let go and allow You to completely heal every area of my life. I know fear does not come from You, so help me to move beyond my fears and walk in faith. If I am missing something that You are trying to reveal to me open my eyes that I may see and open my ears that I may hear. I want every good thing that You have to give me and every plan for my life to be fulfilled, and I know in order to receive I have to have open hands holding onto nothing but You. Help me to take off my grave cloths and walk away free. I love You Lord,

                                                             Amen.

~ Lesson 11 ~

The Exchange

Prayer-

    Thank you Lord that You are the same yesterday, today, and forever. I am thankful I can always count on You and Your promises. When everything around me is changing, You are my constant. Help me to keep my mind focused on You and the plans You have for my life and not my own ideas or hang ups. Give me strength to keep pushing ahead and not to settle. In the name of Jesus.   Amen.

You have been going through so much emotional, spiritual, and mental anguish. Your faith has been tested, your emotions have been pushed to the limit, your mind has been on overload; yet here you still are. You are also stronger than you have ever been. You have a quiet strength that runs deep. You are more humble now than you have ever been. I want to encourage you not to lose this. You are more reflective with life in general, but also about God. You have been still more than ever, yet your thoughts have also been as numerous as the stars. God is picking you up right now and placing you on the Rock. You are in the process of being transformed. You cannot stop here.

Read Ephesians 1:4-5. What does this mean to you?

_____

_____

_____

_____

Kristi Lemley

God has chosen you for such a time as this. Keep pushing forward. You cannot stop. There is one last step you must complete. It is called an exchange. You must completely give God your brokenness and He will give you His beauty.

Read Isaiah 61:1-3. What do these verses mean to you?

_____
_____
_____
_____

God wants to take your brokenness and give you beauty.

God wants to take your brokenness and give you the oil of joy.

God wants to take your brokenness and give you the garment of praise.

This is the phase where you begin to realize you will never be the same. Your trial is going to turn into a testimony. Your mess will become a ministry.

Read Jeremiah 29:11. What does it mean to you?

_____
_____
_____
_____

God wants to do amazing things in and through you. Take time right now and pray. Ask God to speak to your heart and reveal to you the plans He has for you.

Broken and Transformed Workbook

What is God speaking to your heart right now? _____

_____

_____

_____

Can you imagine these plans? If yes, why? If no, why not? _____

_____

_____

_____

_____

_____

Here is where I am going to encourage you to push one last time. It is like having a baby. You are going through labor. You are exhausted, you look a mess, and you have been gritting your teeth, holding onto the bedrails for support, probably yelling, and maybe even spitting (nice picture isn't it?). However, the doctor says, "One more push. I can see the head. It will all be over with one more push." That is what I am saying to you right now. PUSH! Push past this one last thing. Lay down your brokenness at the cross and walk away beautiful.

Read Philippians 1:6. What does it mean to you?

_____

_____

_____

_____

God will complete what He began in you.

There are other character traits that are also being developed in you right now that will help you fulfill the plans God has for you.

Read Galatians 5:22-23. What does it mean to you?

_____
_____
_____
_____

For your situation-

How has love grown in you? _____
_____
_____

How has joy grown in you? _____
_____
_____

How has peace grown in you? _____
_____
_____

How has patience grown in you? _____
_____
_____

Broken and Transformed Workbook

How has kindness grown in you? _____

_____

_____

How has goodness grown in you? _____

_____

_____

How has faithfulness grown in you? _____

_____

_____

How has gentleness grown in you? _____

_____

_____

How has self control grown in you? _____

_____

_____

Read James 1:2-4. What does it mean to you?

_____

_____

_____

How can you make sure that the situation you went through has strengthened you so you may be developed?

_____

_____

Read Romans 5:3-8. What does it mean to you?

_____

_____

_____

_____

I love what Paul say in Philippians 3:13-14. Read it and then write what it means to you.

_____

_____

_____

_____

How do you push and make the exchange? Continue to run to God. Give Him your pain, negative emotions, negative thoughts, and difficult times. Then, allow His peace, love, and goodness to flow to you.

David was anointed king at an early age, but it was many years before it ever happened. He became depressed, angry, and discouraged, but kept going to God. In Acts 13:22 it comments that David was a man after God's own heart. How did David make the exchange? Read the Psalms. Praise and worship. What do you need to do in order to make the exchange? _____

_____

Broken and Transformed Workbook

What is keeping you from making the exchange? _____

_____

_____

Is there anyone who is discouraging you from making the exchange? Who?

_____

How are they discouraging you from making the exchange? _____

_____

_____

Joseph had many dreams of greatness, yet he went through many years of slavery and as a prisoner. (Genesis 37-40) How did he make the exchange from bondage to the second in command of all Egypt?

Read Genesis 45:5-8. He focused on God's plan for His life and forgiveness. You need to focus on what God has in store for you and forgive anyone who you need to forgive.

Read Galatians 6:9. What does it mean to you?

_____

_____

_____

_____

Keep pushing toward the exchange. It is coming. Can you sense it? Before long, you will be able to state the same words Paul stated in Galatians 2:20.

Kristi Lemley

Read Galatians 2:20. What does it mean to you?

_____
_____
_____

Keep repeating this verse until you believe it in your innermost being. Are you becoming more beautiful? Have you exchanged your ashes for His beauty? For some of you, this will be a process in itself. It will take crying out to God on a daily basis for a while for His help. But hang in there. Your beauty will come. For others, I can already see the gray of your life turning into a beautiful array of colored gemstones.

What is one thing you have learned in this lesson that has been helpful?

_____
_____
_____
_____

Prayer-

   Thank you Lord for making me beautiful. Help me to see myself as beautiful and nothing less. Help me to give everything about my situation to You, and when I want to hold on to the mess encourage me to let it go. Help me to keep coming to You over and over until I am transformed. Help me to allow Your grace to cover my life, situation, and future. I know there are days that I am able to have hope and see a better tomorrow, but there are other days that everything still seems so overwhelming. I know You are working in my life because I feel it, sense it, and see it. Thank you that You have not given up on me and have been patient with me. I love You Lord,   Amen.

CONCLUSION

Psalm 126:5, "THEY WHO SOW IN TEARS SHALL REAP IN JOY AND SINGING."

~ Lesson 12 ~

A Time of Refreshing

Prayer-

     Thank you Lord for Your grace and love. You are a good God and You never take Your eyes off of me. I am thankful that You are mindful about everything happening in my life- big and small, new and old. I cannot tell You how much I love You and words cannot describe what You mean to me. Thank you for being right beside me throughout this journey and I know that You have plans for my life to bless me. Help me to receive everything You have to give me. In the name of Jesus,

          Amen.

You have been reading for a while now and hopefully you have absorbed what you read. I pray that God has spoken to you through the book and workbook so far and you find yourself in a place of peace. Your circumstances may not have changed greatly yet, but you know it is just a matter of time before they do.

Your appreciation for God has grown so deep. You have rawness to your relationship with God that was not present before. I know, I have been there. Everything has a beginning and ending. The only thing that does not is God. He is forever! You can trust Him, count on Him, lean on Him, and cry out to Him.

Read Ecclesiastes 3:1-8. What do these verses mean to you?

_____

_____

Kristi Lemley

_____

_____

The time for mourning and being broken will end. I know, remember I have been there. A time of refreshing is going to come. Maybe it has already begun. Keep your eyes on God and watch what He will do.

Read Romans 8:18, 28-31. What do these verses mean to you?

_____

_____

_____

_____

God is for you. He has always been for you. He has never been mad at you. I know some people think God is mad at them, but He isn't! God can and will turn everything into a benefit for you. Just like God turned my trial into a book, He will turn your situation into a blessing. Somehow. Someway.

Are you ready for a time of refreshing? _____

Read Acts 3:19. What does it mean to you?

_____

_____

_____

_____

Broken and Transformed Workbook

You are recovering from the effects of your situation. God will give you new life, new strength, and possibly even a new direction for your life.

Read Philippians 4:12. What does it mean to you?

_____
_____
_____
_____

Learning to be content is very difficult in the storm. Learning to be content after the storm can be even more difficult. What do you think is making it difficult for you to be content right now? _____

_____
_____

Take time to enjoy life by spending time with family and friends or by doing activities that make you laugh. Do not feel guilty to enjoy life again! What can you do to enjoy life right now? _____

_____
_____

What can you do to continue to spend time with God? _____

_____
_____

One reason refreshing times come is to fill you up again. This is in order to be used and poured out to bless others. Like the Israelites celebrated after entering the Promised Land, they then had to focus on obtaining the Promised Land by conquering the inhabitants. Enjoy the refreshing times because they will not last forever. However, they will last long enough for you to feel completely refreshed and rejuvenated in order for you to reach out to others.

Read II Corinthians 1:3-4. What do these verses mean to you?

_____
_____
_____
_____

The wisdom you have gained from your situation can be shared with others. Have you ever wondered why people are drawn to other people spiritually? It is because deep calls out to deep. In other words, the spirit is leading you to them because you need to hear what they have to say.

Do you have any lasting guilt? If so, take it to the Lord so refreshing times will abound. Remember, God has a plan for your life. He is not mad at you. He loves you more than anything and He wants to continue to pour Himself into your life. Receive! Just sit still and receive all that God has to give and offer you. Know that you are never alone. No, never!

Sit still right now and ask God to shower you with His presence and whatever gifts you need. What do you sense at this time? _____

_____
_____
_____

Broken and Transformed Workbook

What all has God done for you? _____

_____

_____

_____

What have you learned about God through everything you have been through?

_____

_____

_____

_____

_____

_____

What have you learned about yourself? _____

_____

_____

_____

_____

_____

What wisdom do you have to give to others? _____

_____

_____

_____

_____

As you move forward, remember how beautiful you are and there really is beauty in being broken.

Kristi Lemley

What is one thing you have learned this lesson that has been helpful?

_____

_____

_____

Prayer-

      Thank you Lord for refreshing my life and giving me a renewed sense of purpose. I know everything that I have been through will someday bring hope and healing to someone else, so continue to complete in me what You began. I know everything that happens has to go through Your hands and You know what I am capable of handling with Your help. Help me to enjoy every day of my life and not take life for granted. I pray that Your joy and peace shine through me to a hurting world that they may see You. I love You Lord,

                                                                                   Amen.

Letter from Kristi-

Thank you for taking this journey with me. I pray that your life is transformed into something beautiful. I want to encourage you to continue to read and study in the areas that you still struggle with. If forgiveness remains an issue, then go back over the lesson and spend more time in prayer asking God to help you. If letting go of everything and moving forward is difficult ask God to help you take off your grave cloths. Whatever area is a struggle, keep going over that lesson and pray until there is victory. Victory WILL come. Take time and allow God to heal you completely.

May God continue to bless you, keep you in His care, and shine His face upon you. May He also grant you His peace. I would love to hear from you. Visit the website at kristilemley.com and click the contact us button.

Much love,

Kristi

Made in the USA
Charleston, SC
13 December 2012